THINK LIKE A SCIENTIST!

Written by
Susan Martineau

Designed & illustrated by
Vicky Barker

CONTENTS

www.bsmall.co.uk

Published by b small publishing ltd. www.bsmall.co.uk © b small publishing ltd. 2021 • 1 2 3 4 5 •
ISBN-13 (Print): 978-1-913918-09-5   ISBN -13 (ePDF): 978-1-913918-10-1
Publisher: Sam Hutchinson.   Art director: Vicky Barker.   Editorial: Sam Hutchinson & Jenny Jacoby.   Printed in China by WKT Co. Ltd.

Science is Everywhere!

Science helps us to find out about everything around us on our beautiful planet, and beyond into the Universe. It also helps us to live safe and healthy lives.

What is a black hole in space?

Where will there be another earthquake?

What lives in the deepest depths of the oceans?

Do trees talk to each other?

How many lemurs are left in the wild?

Scientists are never finished with their work. They are always finding out new things and they do this by asking lots of questions, experimenting, observing and then asking more questions.

Why and how did that happen?

When did it happen?

Can we measure or test that?

Will it happen again?

How can we find out more?

What is that made of?

We also need to ask questions to understand what scientists tell us, and to navigate this world of scientific information and evidence. If we ask the right questions we can learn more about how they do their work.

Asking questions is the best way to find out true facts. There is always more to find out so maybe you will become a scientist yourself, too!

Activity

Think about some science news that has intrigued, excited, or perhaps worried you recently. Make a list of the questions you want to ask to find out more about it.

Word to Know

EVIDENCE is anything that helps to prove that something is, or is not, true.

3

What Do Scientists Actually Do?

Scientists are like explorers finding out about the world and everything in it. They ask loads of questions, but how do they find out the answers?

Scientists come up with a possible answer to their question. This is called a ...

HYPOTHESIS.

It does not matter if it is right or wrong. It is something they can now **TEST**.

Scientists **TEST** the hypothesis by doing experiments, measuring or observing things. They might even have to make new equipment especially for their experiment.

The results might, or might not, back up the hypothesis. They often end up with even more questions and need to do more experiments!

Scientists look at their results and **EVALUATE** them.

Activity

Design your own experiment or try this eggsperiment!

The question

What could make an egg float?

The hypothesis

If I add salt to warm water, an egg will float in it.

Equipment (or apparatus)

Two large clear jars, two uncooked eggs, 1 tablespoon, lots of salt

Method

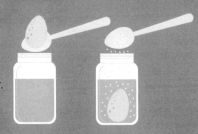

Fill both jars with very warm water from the tap.
Gently lower an egg into each one.
Then stir several spoonfuls of salt into one beaker.

Observe and note what happens!

What conclusions can you draw from the results?
What happens if you repeat the experiment? Is there any way of improving or changing the way you did this activity if you were to do it again?

(See page 31 for an Eggsplanation.)

Was it a fair test?

This is when only one thing is changed (called the variable) during an experiment and everything else is kept the same. In this experiment the variable is the salt being added to just one beaker. The water and egg stay the same for both.

Words to Know

EVALUATE means to weigh up or judge the results of an experiment.

A **CONCLUSION** is what you decide is true after looking carefully at all the evidence or results.

5

How Did They Find That Out?

Do you ever wonder just how scientists have worked out some of the most amazing and interesting animal facts we read about?

How speedy is a cheetah?

Cheetahs have been timed running at amazing speeds in zoos, but what about in the wild?

Scientists attached special tracking collars to five cheetahs in Botswana, Africa. They tracked the animals for 17 months and carefully worked through all the data they collected. They discovered that, when hunting, the cheetahs accelerated faster than most cars, going from zero to 60 mph (96 kph) in just 3 seconds!

How many lemurs are left in the wild?

Many species of lemur are in danger of extinction because the forests they live in are being cut or burnt down. But can scientists actually work out how many are left in the wild?

Lemurs live in the remote areas of Madagascar and they are really hard to spot. Scientists had the clever idea of also counting the trees that lemurs like to eat. They made a 'tree map' using the data they collected. This helped them to estimate how many lemurs there probably were in different parts of the forest. It showed people how protecting the trees also helps the lemurs.

Can crows use tools to get fast food?

Crows have been spotted in the wild using sticks to dig bugs out of tree bark, but just how clever are they?

Scientists set up a nifty test for eight Caledonian crows in a laboratory. They did not train them beforehand. The crows were shown a box with a tasty snack in it, along with some bits of stick and thin tubes. All of the birds worked out how to put these together to make a tool to poke the food out of the box!

What questions do you think the scientists asked?

HOW CAN WE DO THIS?

Words to Know

DATA is a collection of facts or information, like measurements, numbers, or observations. It is a Latin word and, when used in science, is plural. You say 'the data show ... ' not 'shows'.

ANALYSE means to look at or study something in detail to understand or find out what it means.

CREATIVE PLANNING

OBSERVATION (lots!)

RECORDING DATA

Activity

CHECKING AND ANALYSING DATA

Some birds hop and some walk when they are on the ground. Can you plan an experiment to observe and record this behaviour? Can you also analyse your data to identify which birds hop and which ones walk?

WHAT DOES THIS INFORMATION TELL US?

They also needed **DETERMINATION** when clambering through a Madagascan forest!

Science to the Rescue

When there is a natural disaster, such as an earthquake or volcanic eruption, scientists use all their scientific knowledge and skills to become disaster detectives. It is like doing an experiment backwards, because they can already see the results.

Why did the ground shake?

What caused that eruption?

Why was there a tsunami?

Saving lives

If scientists can understand why a disaster has happened, they might be able to predict if, when and where it might happen again. They can also help people who live in danger zones to prepare and become more resilient for the future.

Earthquake-resistant buildings

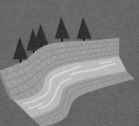

Flood defences

EVACUATION ROUTE

Early-warning systems for tsunamis

Seismologists are scientists who study earthquakes. They track and measure the movements of the giant slabs of rock that make up Earth's surface.

Volcanologists study volcanoes. They try to predict when and how volcanoes will erupt.

The Mysterious Exploding Lake

21 August 1986
Over 1,700 people died near Lake Nyos in Cameroon, Africa.

What did the scientists discover?

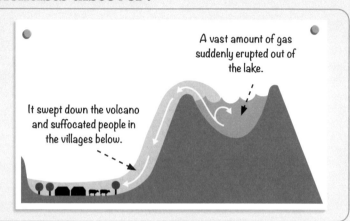

The lake is in an old volanic crater. Carbon dioxide (CO_2) builds up at the bottom of the lake.

It swept down the volcano and suffocated people in the villages below.

A vast amount of gas suddenly erupted out of the lake.

Can they prevent another similar disaster?

Teams of scientists have put special tubes in the lake to release the gas and to stop such deadly amounts of it building up again.

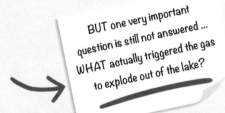

BUT one very important question is still not answered ... WHAT actually triggered the gas to explode out of the lake?

Activity

You could investigate the science behind another disaster you have read or heard about. What caused the disaster and might it be prevented from happening again? Is there anything we still don't understand about it yet?

Words to Know

RESILIENT means able to survive difficult conditions or recover quickly after a disaster.

CARBON DIOXIDE is the gas we breathe out and it is in the atmosphere around us. Normal amounts of it will not harm you.

Which Scientist to Ask

There are so many different kinds of scientific work that there is probably a scientist working right now on some of the questions you might want to ask and the facts you would like to know.

Activity

Can you match the scientist to these questions? (Answers on page 31.)
You could think of some other questions and find out which scientist might know the answers. You might want to consult more than one, because scientists also often work together.

A. Ornithologist
B. Astronomer
C. Epidemiologist
D. Oceanographer
E. Palaeontologist

↖ (can you say that out loud?)

1. What is a black hole in space?

2. How much plastic rubbish is there in the sea?

Scientists don't always agree
Scientists sometimes come up with different theories, or ideas, to explain results or evidence.

About 1.2 billion years ago, a massive meteorite smashed down in Scotland, but the geologists (rock scientists) who have investigated this don't agree on exactly where it landed. It might have been where the sea is now, or in a place called Lairg. In Lairg the pull of gravity is slightly lower than elsewhere. This kind of difference can be the result of a space-rock impact.

3. How far do migrating birds fly?

5. What is causing this disease to spread?

4. Is that a dinosaur bone or something a dog just buried?

YAY!

In theory, the schoolchildren of Lairg can jump just a tiny bit higher than their friends down the road!

Words to Know

GRAVITY is the force that pulls everything on Earth towards the centre of the planet.

A **BLACK HOLE** forms after a star has exploded. It has such a huge pull of gravity that it sucks light into it and also disturbs the flow of time, making time run more slowly the nearer it gets to the hole.

Science in the News

Science stories pop up in the news every day. They can make us feel excited, scared or curious. What questions do we need to ask to find out the true facts of the science behind the headlines?

TORNADO TERROR Forecast!

DOGS CAN READ OUR MINDS!

WHO
is writing or sharing this news?

WHERE
did they get this information?

WHAT
is the scientific evidence behind the story?

Is it old or new information?

How do we know if it is fake or not-quite-true news?

TESTS REVEAL LEFT-HANDED PEOPLE ARE SMARTER!

CHILDREN BORN TODAY WILL LIVE UNTIL THEY ARE 100!!!

Beware of the share!

Science stories are often shared on social media. But the information might not be true or only tell part of the story. The person writing it might not understand the information, or even deliberately misrepresent it. Perhaps they are only picking out the bits that agree with what they already believe or want to say.

GET THE FACTS STRAIGHT!

How would you feel if you were a scientist who had discovered something really amazing only for it to be shared inaccurately by other people?

Activity

Find a science story in the news and compare the way it is presented across several news sources. You could then research and verify the science behind the story to find out the facts for yourself. See page 32 for more on how to do this.

Words to Know

VERIFY means to check that something is true or correct.

MISREPRESENT means to twist information so that people do not get the true facts.

What is This Information Telling Us?

Some scientists carry out experiments in the form of studies or surveys. They might be testing a new medicine, researching insects in a particular habitat, or seeing if people can tell the difference between real meat and some they have made in a laboratory.

They end up with a lot of numbers and information to crunch through.

They have to analyse it all and work out what it means.

What connections and patterns can they see?

Activity

Be a citizen scientist! There are lots of surveys and studies that need your help. Have a look online to find something you would like to get involved with. You could collect weather data, do a frog watch, observe birds and butterflies, or even be an astronomer looking at images of faraway galaxies. Remember to check with an adult before signing up to anything online and keep all your personal information private.

There are some important questions to ask about any study or survey.

HOW BIG WAS IT?
How many people took part? How big an area was surveyed? The bigger the study, the more reliable the results will usually be.

HOW QUICKLY WAS IT DONE?
Scientists may be under pressure to find results. Any early news about results will probably not be the final word. More research and studies may be needed to validate their work.

WHO CARRIED IT OUT?
Were they specialists in the area of the study? Did several scientists all work together? Perhaps a series of surveys was done across the world so that they could compare results?

WHO PAID FOR IT?
Was it an independent study? For example, if a burger survey was paid for by the company making them, then this needs to be made clear.

BUT always remember that it is really important for any researcher or scientist **NOT** to assume they know what the answers will be before they have done their research.

Words to Know

RELIABLE describes information, or people, you can believe or trust.

VALIDATE means to confirm or prove that something is accurate and true.

How to Read Like a Scientist

Scientific information is often shown using infographics like graphs, charts and tables. They should be clear and easy to understand, but it still takes practice to 'read' them.

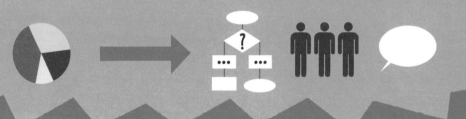

Hopefully, these infographics are not confusing at all! Can you understand what they are trying to show? You could try reading them out loud.

How far does the snail travel in a day?

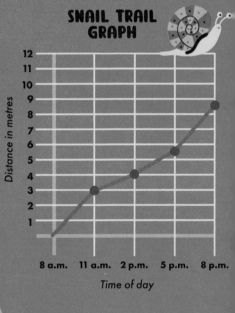

SNAIL TRAIL GRAPH

Distance in metres

12
11
10
9
8
7
6
5
4
3
2
1

8 a.m.　11 a.m.　2 p.m.　5 p.m.　8 p.m.

Time of day

FAVOURITE PIZZA TOPPINGS IN MR MOZZARELLA'S COOKERY CLASS

- red peppers
- pepperoni
- ham
- mozzarella
- cherry tomatoes
- olives

This pie chart is showing me that the most popular topping is pepperoni ... and the least favourite is olives.

Thinking is hard work!

The brain uses 20% (one fifth) of your energy, which is quite a lot for a small part of your body!

Don't rush!

Reading and looking at information needs to be done carefully. Do some slow thinking instead of quickly assuming you know what it is telling you. It is worth taking your time to understand something.

Activity

Line graphs are a great way to show changes that happen over time. Can you show the following information so that it is clear to anyone reading it? Or you could make up your own graph using data you have gathered yourself.

* At the beginning of Week 1, the puppy was born. It weighed 300 g.

* By Week 2, it weighed 600 g.

* For the next three weeks it put on 400 g each week.

Word to Know

INFOGRAPHICS show us information using pictures as well as words and numbers.

(See page 31 for a Puppy Line Graph.)

The Language of Science

Scientists write about their work and display their results using a language that other scientists can understand. They can then repeat experiments or compare results. As soon as we start learning science at school, we are learning the language, too!

Using standard units of measurement is really important.

Millimetres, centimetres, metres, kilometres

height/length/distance

Newtons

force

Degrees Celsius (°C)

temperature

Seconds, minutes, hours

time

How do measurements relate to each other?

Scientists use handy formulae to show how measurements relate to each other. Here's one for working out the average speed of something:

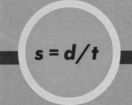

$$s = d/t$$

s means speed

d means distance travelled

t means time taken

The average speed equals the distance travelled, divided by the time taken. Nifty and easy to remember! It is why we talk about speed as kilometres (or miles) per hour.

Distance = 20 km   **Time** = 2 hours

A light year is a measurement of distance.

It is how far light travels in a year.

1 light year is about 9.5 trillion km (5.9 trillion miles). The light of the Sun takes only 8 minutes to reach Earth so imagine how far it goes in a year!

1 TRILLION = a million millions = 1 with 12 zeros after it!

Is there a scientific name for everything?

Every known living thing on Earth is named following rules that every scientist across the world follows. It is a system that was started in the eighteenth century when Latin and Greek were the international languages of science.

LATIN

Scientific name		Common name
Canis	familiarus	Dog
Canis	lupus	Grey wolf
Canis	latrans	Coyote

Genus — Canis ... — Species

GREEK

Giga	a thousand million	1,000,000,000
Nano	a thousand millionth	1/1,000,000,000

This is helpful shorthand for when there are so many zeros.

Activity

Can you work out the speed of the bicycle in kilometres per hour?
(See the answer on page 31.)

Word to Know

FORMULAE is the plural (more than one) of **FORMULA**. These are ways of showing, or working out, how pieces of information like measurements relate to each other.

Is it OK to Do That Experiment?

Whatever scientists are working on, it is important for them, and us, to ask if their experiments will cause any harm. This is sometimes a very difficult question to answer.

Famously dodgy, but amazingly effective!

In 1796 Edward Jenner, an English doctor, carried out a dangerous experiment. He took some cowpox germs and inserted them into the arms of several children, including his own baby son. Then he deliberately infected them with a dreadful disease called smallpox!

The cowpox germs stopped the children from getting smallpox, which was similar to cowpox but much more deadly. Thanks to Jenner this was a medical breakthrough that he called '**vaccination**'.
But his experiment would never be allowed now.
It was unethical.

'Vacca' is the Latin word for 'cow'.

Why was it unethical?

Jenner's experiment could have badly harmed the children, if not actually killed them! They certainly had no idea of the danger they were in and had not agreed to take such a risk.

What about experiments on animals?

These are carried out to develop new drugs and test the safety of other products like cosmetics. But is it ethical? Can it ever be all right to hurt animals even if it means scientists find a new and amazing medicine?

Is it worse to **DO** these experiments than **NOT DO** them and possibly harm humans by not finding this medicine?

You could have a debate with your friends or family on the following questions, or you could conduct a survey of friends and family to see if they answer 'yes' or 'no' to them. Write up a contract for them to sign to say that they are happy to take part in this survey.

1. Do you think it is ever all right to conduct experiments on animals?

2. Would you volunteer for a research programme testing a new drug?

Words to Know

UNETHICAL describes someone or something that breaks the proper safe and responsible rules of scientific work.

CONSENT means agreement or permission to do something.

CONSENT FORM FOR SURVEY VOLUNTEERS

All information and answers will remain confidential.

I confirm that I am taking part voluntarily in this survey and understand that I may withdraw at any time.

FULL NAME:

SIGNATURE:

DATE:

Keeping an Open Mind

Sometimes scientists find something completely unexpected during their work, or their results inspire a new invention. This is another reason why scientists need to keep asking questions all the time.

Why did that happen when I did not predict it?

What is the connection between these results?

Have I found something world-changing?

Smart dust

In 2003, a chemistry student called Jamie Link was experimenting with tiny silicon chips when one of them burst into even more teeny pieces. She was amazed to discover that they could still work as miniscule sensors.

Not just any old mould!

Bacteria are tiny organisms and some of them can make us ill. In 1928, Alexander Fleming observed something unusual when he was experimenting with bacteria. One of his samples accidentally ended up with mould on it and Fleming saw that bacteria did not grow near it. The mould was penicillin, an antibiotic that many of us will have taken to treat a bacterial infection.

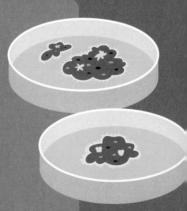

The unsquishable bug!
The diabolical ironclad beetle can survive being run over by a car. That is like being crushed by 39,000 times its own weight. Researchers 3-D scanned it at the same time as trying to squash it. Thankfully it was not harmed! Its wing cases have interlocking, jigaw-like pieces which make it superhero tough. Scientists can now develop similar ways of joining different materials, like plastic and metal, to make aircraft or buildings much stronger.

Weird weather
The catastrophic volcanic eruption of Krakatau in 1883 caused extreme changes in the world's weather and skies. Meteorologists realised that volcanic ash was travelling around Earth high up in the atmosphere. They had discovered the jet stream, a band of very strong winds that whooshes around our planet, several kilometres up in the atmosphere.

Science in space
The International Space Station (ISS) is like a laboratory in orbit around our planet. Many of the experiments are designed to find out if humans could ever really live in space, and travel further into the Universe.

Activity

Word to Know

A **SILICON CHIP** is a tiny piece of silicon inside a computer. It contains electronic circuits and can store loads of information or do complicated calculations.

You can track and spot the ISS in the night sky as it travels overhead. Just download one of the space station-spotting apps to find out when it will pass near to you.

Pioneers in Medicine

We often read about amazing new medical advances, like vaccines and new treatments. But how can we be sure they are safe? What questions do scientists ask to make sure?

What is a vaccine?

A vaccine makes the body's own immune system produce antibodies that can fight off germs that cause disease. It is especially important for diseases caused by viruses, because these cannot be treated with antibiotics (see page 22). Vaccines save millions of lives.

How do they make sure a vaccine is safe?

Testing on **animals**.

Does it work in the laboratory?

Testing on a small group of up to **100 humans**.

All the humans are **VOLUNTEERS**.

Is it safe for humans? Does it work? Are there any side effects?

Testing on **several hundred humans**.

How do human immune systems react to the vaccine? Are there any side effects?

Viruses are smaller than bacteria. They cause diseases like chickenpox and Covid-19. They cannot be treated with antibiotics.

Words to Know

An **ANTIBODY** is a substance that our bodies can make. Antibodies travel in our blood to destroy other substances that carry illnesses.

ERADICATE means to get rid of completely.

Killer disease

In 1967, the deadly disease smallpox killed 2 million people. By 1979 the disease had been eradicated by worldwide vaccination.

Amazing Alice

Alice Ball was a chemistry professor at the University of Hawaii. In 1916 she discovered a new way to treat people suffering from a terrible skin disease called leprosy. This transformed their lives. Sadly, she died at a young age and was not recognised for her pioneering work for many decades.

Testing on **thousands of humans**.

They are either given the vaccine or a placebo (something that has no medical effect) to compare results between them.

Independent organisations in charge of making sure vaccines and medicines are safe doublecheck the scientists' results. They decide if it is safe to offer the vaccine to everyone.

Are there any rare side effects we haven't spotted yet? How well does the vaccine work on this much larger group of people?

Activity

How much do you know about how your body works every day? Do you know where your heart, lungs, liver and stomach are located? Can you find out the different names of your digestive system and track the path of your breakfast through your body?

(See page 31 for answers.)

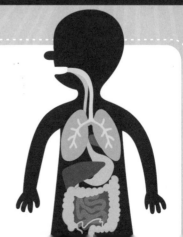

Will We Ever Know EVERYTHING?

The short answer to this question is 'no'! And the more we know, the more we know we don't know! Even things that we think we know now could change as scientists carry on their work.

SCIENTIFIC PROGRESS

New discoveries and information as long as scientists keep asking questions and experimenting.

We all need to keep asking questions, too.
But most of us have done that since we learned to talk!

Why did that happen?

When was this discovered?

What is the most up-to-date information or research?

Humans like to find the reasons for why things happen. But we need to avoid

SPECULATION.

This means opinions or theories that are not backed up by scientific evidence.

... our incredible brains?

Neuroscientists use technology called fMRI scanning (functional Magnetic Resonance Imaging) to map which bits of our brain we use for different activities. But there is still so much we do not understand about how our brains work – yet!

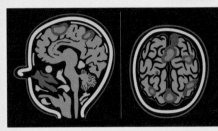

... the mysterious creatures of the oceans?

More than 80% (four fifths) of our oceans have not been explored so scientists still do not know how many species exist in the deep. How tragic it would be if we never learn about some of them because climate change wipes them out before they are found.

... the astonishing ecosystems of forests?

Under every forest floor there is a complicated, underground network of fungi that connects trees to each other through their roots. Trees can share nutrients through this amazing Wood Wide Web, so it helps to keep the whole forest healthy. Scientists have started to map networks across the world to understand how climate change affects the different fungi and their forests.

Activity

You could make a timeline of a scientific discovery that inspires you. Find out the most recent facts about it. Maybe there will be future developments, too.

Word to Know

NEUROSCIENTISTS study everything about our brains and nervous systems. The word 'neuro' comes from the Greek 'neuron' which means 'nerve'.

27

Science of the Imagination

Sometimes the first step to finding out something new in science is to ask some rather mind-boggling questions that stretch our imagination. It is like setting yourself a very tricky puzzle to work out or test an idea.

Will humans ever be able to time-travel?
One brilliant theory suggests wormholes in the Universe are like shortcuts through space and time. Anything travelling through a wormhole would move faster than the speed of light and travel through time!

What is the smallest particle in the Universe?
For now, scientists think the smallest particles are quarks, but this is just what their experiments using the latest equipment have discovered. One day, new technology will help us to find even titchier ones!

electron

nucleus

quark

proton

neutron

Quarks are found inside protons and neutrons, inside atoms.

Imaginary worlds

The scientist Albert Einstein did what he called 'thought experiments'. But this doesn't mean he was trying to become a mind-reader. He imagined experiments that you could never do in real life, like running as fast as a beam of light!

Fiction to fact

In 1983, the science-fiction author Isaac Asimov foresaw the use of robotics in factories and offices. He also predicted that children would learn everything they needed to know from computers. They would still need teachers to inspire them to be curious, though!

Arthur C. Clarke wrote about satellites and communication gadgets he called 'personal transceivers' in 1959. This was long before the invention of the mobile phone.

Activity

Make a time capsule. Write a list of the most up-to-date gadgets you can think of and find some pictures of them. Include your scientific predictions for the future, too. Put them in a container with your name and date and hide them at the back of a cupboard. You can look at them in a few years' time. (If you don't forget where the capsule is!)

Words to Know

PARTICLES are extremely small pieces of matter. They are like tiny building blocks that make up everything in the Universe.

ROBOTICS means designing and building machines (**robots**) to make things or do certain, very repetitive, jobs that humans usually do.

Words to Know

analyse means to look at or study something in detail to understand or find out what it means.

antibiotics are medicines used to treat infections caused by bacteria. They do not work against viruses.

antibody is a substance that our bodies can make. Antibodies travel in our blood to destroy other substances that carry illnesses.

apparatus is the equipment you use to do experiments.

bacterium is a tiny, invisible organism. Bacteria is the word for more than one. Some bacteria cause diseases. These can be treated with antibiotics.

black hole forms after a star has exploded. It has such a huge pull of gravity that it sucks light into it and also disturbs the flow of time, making time run more slowly the nearer it gets to the hole.

carbon dioxide is the gas we breathe out and it is in the atmosphere around us. Normal amounts of it will not harm you.

conclusion is what you decide is true after looking carefully at all the evidence or results.

consent means agreement or permission to do something.

data is a collection of facts or information, like measurements, numbers, or observations. It is a Latin word and, when used in science, is plural. You say 'the data show...' not 'shows'.

eradicate means to get rid of completely.

estimate means to roughly count or judge the numbers of something.

evaluate means to weigh up or judge the results of an experiment.

evidence is anything that helps to prove that something is, or is not, true.

formulae is the plural (more than one) of **formula**. These are ways of showing, or working out, how pieces of information like measurements relate to each other.

gravity is the force that pulls everything on Earth towards the centre of the planet. Gravity is what gives us weight and makes things fall to the ground.

hypothesis is an explanation for something that can be tested to see if it is true.

infographics are a way of showing information using pictures as well as words and numbers.

misrepresent means to twist information so that people do not get the true facts.

neuroscientists study everything about our brains and nervous systems. The word 'neuro' comes from the Greek 'neuron' which means 'nerve'.

particles are extremely small pieces of matter. They are like tiny building blocks that make up everything in the Universe.

placebo is a substance that has no medical effect.

reliable describes information, or people, you can believe or trust.

resilient means able to survive difficult conditions or recover quickly after a disaster.

robotics means designing and building machines (robots) to make things or do certain very repetitive or precise jobs that humans usually do.

side effect is an unwanted, sometimes unpleasant, result or symptom.

silicon chip is a tiny piece of silicon inside a computer. It contains electronic circuits and can store loads of information or do complicated calculations.

speculation is when we, or other people, come up with opinions or theories that are not backed up by scientific evidence.

unethical describes someone or something that breaks the proper safe and responsible rules of scientific work.

vaccination is a treatment that gets our own bodies to protect us against diseases.

validate means to confirm or prove that something is accurate and true.

variable is one thing that is changed during an experiment.

verify means to check that something is true or correct.

virus is a tiny, invisible organism that is smaller than a bacterium. It causes diseases like colds, chickenpox and Covid-19. These cannot be treated with antibiotic medicine.

Answers to Activities

page 5
An egg in unsalted water is denser than the water so it does not float. When salt is added to water it makes the water denser than an egg. Therefore an egg will float in saltwater.

pages 10-11 1.B; 2.D; 3.A; 4.E; 5.C.

page 17

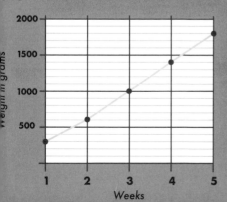

pages 18-19
The speed of the bicycle is 10 kph (kilometres per hour).

page 25

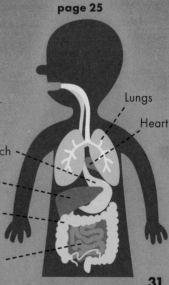

Lungs

Heart

Stomach

Liver

Large intestine

Small intestine

31

Be a Scientist!

What kind of scientist would you like to be? Perhaps you want to help the environment or explore the oceans? Maybe you would like to investigate black holes, invent a new material or discover more about our brilliant brains?

Safe science at home
You could start being a scientist now!

* Plan and design your experiment carefully. (Check with an adult before you start, too.)

* Make sure your experiment is a fair test (see page 5) and record your results clearly.

* Analyse the data. What conclusions can you make from the information?

Remember that scientists **never stop asking questions**! (You can also use big scientific words because you know what they mean now.)

Scientific fact-finding
How do you check the science behind your experiments or the facts about a science story you have read online or in the news?

RESEARCH
information using reliable sources like ...

Encyclopedia and up-to-date books written by specialists.

Websites of academic institutions like universities, specialist organisations like NOAA, the Met Office, NASA, CERN, museums and research stations.

Some of these post information on social media, but check anything you read is from one of these reliable sources first.

REMEMBER ...

WHO
are the scientists behind the information?

CHECK
the dates of the information to make sure you are getting the most up-to-date facts.

CORROBORATE
the facts by looking at more than one source of information.